THE GENUINE ELVIS

THE GENUINE ELVIS
Photos and Untold Stories about the King

Ronnie McDowell, Edie Hand, and Joe Meador

PELICAN PUBLISHING COMPANY

Gretna 2009

B
PresE

---

*The word "Pelican" and the depiction of a pelican are trademarks
of Pelican Publishing Company, Inc., and are registered in the
U.S. Patent and Trademark Office.*

Library of Congress Cataloging-in-Publication Data

McDowell, Ronnie.
  The genuine Elvis : photos and untold stories about the King / Ronnie
McDowell, Edie Hand, and Joe Meador.
      p. cm.
  ISBN 978-1-58980-695-5 (hardcover : alk. paper) 1. Presley, Elvis, 1935-
1977—Anecdotes. 2. Rock musicians—United States—Anecdotes. I. Hand,
Edie, 1951- II. Meador, Joe. III. Title.
  ML420.P96M45 2009
  782.42166092—dc22
  [B]

                                    2009005807

Frontispiece: Elvis Presley on Tommy and Jimmy Dorsey's *Stage Show,* February
1956

Printed in Singapore

Published by Pelican Publishing Company, Inc.
1000 Burmaster Street, Gretna, Louisiana 70053

To all the Elvis fans, because he *rocked* all our worlds.

Timeless, by Ronnie McDowell, 2005

Standing on an old LP record, a young Elvis Presley is surrounded by the Jordanaires as they look today, with a young guitarist Scotty Moore, drummer D.J. Fontana, and bassist Bill Black. Whatever their ages, the men and the music are timeless. This scene is based on an _Ed Sullivan Show_ set, but most fans don't recognize it since the network would only show Elvis and his performers from the waist up due to the way Elvis moved to the music.

Preface

I am so glad to be a part of this collection from family, friends, and fans, and I know you'll treasure the stories, the photos, and Ronnie McDowell's art expressions.

When Ronnie McDowell and Joe Meador asked me to research the possibilities of an insightful, reflective book on Elvis for his fans, I never dreamed the project and these guys would become so special to me. As a cousin to Elvis Presley, it has been my privilege to reveal to all of you insights into the "genuine Elvis" like never before.

Put on your blue suede shoes, slick back your hair, and roll down the windows of your heart. It's a new rock 'n' roll ride for all of you!

Edie Hand
Cousin to the King of Rock 'n' Roll

THE GENUINE ELVIS

"It is rare when an artist's talent can touch an entire generation of people. It's even more rare when that same artist's influence affects several generations in all walks of life. Elvis made an imprint on the world of pop music unequaled by any other single performer."

Dick Clark

Opposite: Elvis at Russwood Park concert after his first appearance on the *Ed Sullivan Show.*

Elvis and his first cousin Gene Smith on the set of *Flaming Star,* 1960.

Louise Smith
Widow of Elvis's Cousin Gene Smith

My experience with Elvis began back in the early '50s. I recall working in a clothing store that offered in-store credit and layaway. My mom also worked there part time on Saturdays. On this particular Saturday, two guys, dressed kind of different from most people of that time, walked into the clothing store. My mother asked one of the boys if he would like to buy a new pair of shoes. He said, "Good gosh, I guess these shoes that I have on would make ol' man Crump sick!" The man he was referring to was our mayor in Memphis at the time and he was in the hospital really ill at that very moment. Everyone in the store began to laugh at this young man's way of responding about his shoes and Mr. Crump.

He went on to pick out some clothes for himself and his friend. He then had to fill out a credit application. I was in charge of getting the information from this young man and his name was Elvis Presley. I got really aggravated with him because every time

that I tried to fill out his application, he would want to know my name and address. Finally, he quit clowning around and I got his credit application handled. I told Elvis he would have to pay on his account once a week. He said, "Fine by me. And my cuz here, Gene Smith, is going to open up an account too."

I recall another Saturday when Elvis and Gene came in the store around lunch and they invited me to go eat at Kay's Diner. Elvis had parked his car down on Beale Street. The street was lined with mostly pawn shops, and Elvis ran ahead of Gene and me to where three big brass balls hung out over the sidewalk. He stopped right under them and started yelling out, "Hurry up, Louise, and kiss me beneath the balls." I could have killed him! Elvis was always up to something.

That memory stands out in my mind so vividly because little did I know that the experience of working in the clothing store would end up leading me to my husband, Gene Smith. We were happily married for forty-three years until his death.

***

When Gene and I began dating back in the '50s, most of the time Elvis was with us. The first time I went out with Gene, he picked me up and there sitting in the back seat of the car was Elvis. I turned to Gene and asked what Elvis was doing there, and Gene's reply was, "I never go anywhere without Cuz," and believe me, he was telling the truth. Whenever you saw one, you would always see the other. The two of them were very close.

We never had the money to do very much when the three of us were on a date, so one of the things we did was ride down Main Street, drive slow, and wait for the light to turn red. We would stop. The guys would open the car doors, stand outside watching until the light turned green, and then they would hop back into the car and drive on down the street. We would always look back and people would be standing in the street wondering what they had just seen. Elvis and Gene would fall out laughing.

Sometimes at night we would go to Kay's Drive-in, park, and sit on the front of the car while Elvis played his guitar. We even had to share one Coke because we didn't have the money to buy three Cokes. Now when people talk about Elvis Presley, they only

think about him being really rich. You see, I was fortunate enough to know the genuine Elvis, the guy who didn't have much money and lived in a housing project. Today when I think about these experiences with Gene and Elvis, I realize we were the richest people in the world.

***

When Gene and Elvis were teenagers, before we were married, they found a grocery store (where Gene later worked delivering groceries), and in this grocery store was an ice-cream shop. They loved going there. They would always order their favorite ice-cream treat, Purple Cows, which was a vanilla ice cream and grape soda mixture. People would laugh at them for always ordering Purple Cows.

***

One year at Christmas (late '50s or early '60s), believe it or not, Gene and I gave Elvis—by that time a very wealthy guy—

Elvis with Col. Tom Parker dressed as Santa Claus on the set of *Wild in the Country*, 1961.

Elvis, second left, and Gene Smith, on right, seated at a table on the *Loving You* movie set.

something he did not own. It was a box filled only with wooden clothes hangers that were wide on the ends so he could hang coats on them. He was like a little kid, and he said, "Okay, this is something I need, and believe it or not, it is something I don't have!" He was so excited about this gift that we did it again and gave him another box of wooden hangers the next Christmas. We got the same reaction. We figured out he just loved Christmas and opening presents.

Of course, after his favorite holiday, Christmas, came the time when he had the most fun, New Year's Eve. He would try to have the biggest fireworks display. His favorite fireworks at the time were the Roman candles, and you would think that there was a war going on in Memphis there were so many colored lights and explosions over his house. I will never forget the fun we had and seeing him so excited at everyone's reaction to the fireworks.

One Christmas, I had just gotten home from the hospital after having back surgery and I couldn't get out of the house to go anywhere. My mom and dad had cooked dinner for us and they brought it to our house so that we could all celebrate Christmas together. As we were sitting down to eat, someone knocked on

our door. It was a Special Delivery man with a thousand-dollar check from Elvis. The card read, "Get well soon, Louise, and Merry Christmas to you, Gene and the kids. Love, Elvis." That is the kind of friend Elvis was to our family.

***

I am sure no one knows that my husband, Gene, and I lived in Elvis's home, Graceland, in the early years. We didn't realize what an honor it was and our bedroom was upstairs next to his bedroom. One funny memory of that time that comes to mind is of Elvis's myna bird. His big cage was in the laundry room at Graceland, right off the kitchen. When the phone would ring, the bird would start yelling, "Hello, hello, Elvis is not here, Elvis is not here." If no one answered the phone, the bird would yell, "All of you get out and go to the devil," and he would say this two or three times. He would also say to anyone that came into the room, "I am Elvis's bird and I am a bad bird." He would also say this if a girl came into his room, and then he would give her a wolf whistle.

***

Roxy Theater, by Ronnie McDowell, 2001. Originally titled *Memories Are Made of This*

The Roxy Theater in Russellville, Alabama, used to show movies like Elvis's *Loving You.* In the foreground Elvis himself drives by in a '57 Ford Fairlane, catching the attention of the girls outside.

Elvis was always renting out theaters, skating rinks, and the Fairgrounds in Memphis for himself and his friends. We would go to the theater about midnight, and he and his girlfriend and Gene and I would always sit in front of the rest of his friends. He would never let anyone sit in front of us or on the row behind us. There were times when he would take a water gun with him, and every now and then, he would hold it where no one could see it and shoot water back at his friends. They would start moving around and looking up to see if the ceiling was leaking. This would go on until his water gun ran out of ammunition, and then he would look at them and laugh.

When Elvis would rent out the skating rink, the girls didn't really get to skate very much because all Elvis wanted to do was show off for the girls. He and the guys would form a long line and "pop the whip" and see which guy they could throw off of the line.

Another one of Elvis's favorite places was the Fairgrounds in Memphis. He loved the bumper cars, and he and the guys would just love to try to run over one another with these little cars. Another ride that he loved was called "the Pippin"; it was a roller coaster, and he and his girlfriend and Gene and I rode it one night thirty-two times without getting off. We just loved spending time with Elvis.

***

One day Elvis came to our house and the press followed him inside. A man and woman accompanied the man from the newspaper. They presented Elvis with a trophy. Written on it was the fact that during Elvis's movies in the theater, they had sold more popcorn than during any other movies. They took a picture of me and Elvis and the woman who presented the trophy, and it was in the newspaper in Memphis. When he left, I told him that he had forgotten his trophy, and he told me that he would get it later. He came over many times to our house, and I always tried to give him the trophy and he always said that he would get it later. Guess what! I still have the trophy that was shown in the newspaper article.

***

Elvis always made sure that we didn't need for anything. One year he took us to Las Vegas so we could see his performances there. He was already in California filming the end of one of his movies, so he flew Gene and I and his girlfriend to California first. Once we got there, he drove us all around Hollywood showing us a lot of different things, and then that night, we left for Las Vegas.

He wanted to get us there before daylight because he wanted to show us all the clubs and all the lights. Of course, we were up all night and we slept all day. Breakfast was always served in our suite, which was a two-bedroom, three-bath unit. We attended his 8 P.M. shows and the other Vegas shows at 12 P.M. He always put us at a front table, and money was no object. We were there for his entire three-and-a-half-week run. We had a ball!

At another time Gene and I were leaving Memphis to drive our children to the Gulf Coast for a week. Something happened to our car before it was time to leave. Gene called Elvis and told him about our car, and Elvis told him not to worry because he was sending a car over so we could go on our trip. *He sent us a limo!* When we called to thank him, he said, "I want you to take your kids in style." You had to know Elvis on a personal level to really know what a great guy he was.

***

In Memphis they used to have gospel singing at the Ellis Auditorium, and you know how much Elvis loved gospel music.

Elvis holds the popcorn trophy, 1956.

Elvis and some of his entourage in Las Vegas.

Elvis, Gene, and I used to go in the back door of the auditorium and go up the stairs. Because there were no lights on upstairs, no one knew that Elvis was there, and no one could see us. We just loved those nights, and sometimes after the show, we would go by Thornton's Doughnut Shop and get milk and hot doughnuts—they tasted so good!

***

I will never forget the day that we found out that Elvis had died. We never thought that anything would ever happen to him because he seemed so strong and he was such a good man. Gene was a pallbearer at his funeral in Memphis.

On March 2, 1999, my husband, Gene, passed away, and I thought that my life was over after being with him for forty-three years. My life was never the same. But now, I live for our daughter, Margaret, and our two sons, Tony and Mike, and our seven grandchildren and six great-grandchildren.

I do hope that these stories will put a little joy and pleasure in your heart. By writing this, I have relived some precious memories in my life, just being with Gene and Elvis.

Elvis in his hotel room in New York City listening to the playback of "Don't Be Cruel."

"Elvis. If you are not a fan, no explanation is possible; if you are an Elvis fan, no explanation is necessary."   George Klein

Charles Watts
Disc Jockey

I met Elvis in Tupelo, Mississippi, in 1956 at the state fairgrounds. My station manager at WTUP selected me to interview Elvis. I remember we were set up in a tent close to the stage, and boy, was it crowded! Elvis was already a big star. I had plenty of tape so I started interviewing his family and friends. First, I interviewed Gladys and Vernon, his mom and dad. Next, I interviewed Nick Adams, who was a Hollywood star and friend of Elvis.

There were so many funny sidebars to the day and night because of the anxious fans. He did a matinee and a night performance. One fan named Judy from Manchester, Tennessee, got through the National Guard, state troopers, county sheriffs, and city police and got up on stage. It took eight good men to subdue her and get her off. So I interviewed her too. The officers promised her they would arrange for her to meet Elvis if she would settle down till after the show. She did, but she kept saying, "I touched Elvis!" Boy, there were all kind of celebrities that year: the Oak Ridge Boys, the

Blackwood Brothers, and the Statesmen. Of course the Jordanaires were backing up Elvis, and he had a good band with him too.

I thought Elvis was so nice to everybody. He was a different kind of person than everyone thought he was. For example, a high-school friends of Elvis was standing in line for an autograph. He didn't think Elvis would remember him after all those years. When Elvis spotted him from way across the tent, he called him and his wife by their first names and said, "Come back here and let's have a Pepsi." He got a photographer to come over and got in the middle of them with his arms around both for a perfect moment for them. That is just the way he was. He was not distracted like many of us would be with all the money he was making. He had already signed a contract, if I am not mistaken, with RCA for a thousand dollars a week, whether he worked or not. He had already made two movies and was working on a third because we talked briefly about that too.

He was almost shy during our interview. In this radio business you don't know who you are going to run into next, but I was delighted to be the one from our station to interview Elvis. It turns out that nobody else had an interview with his mom and his dad and him on the same day. It was a lot of fun!

Elvis and Nick Adams.

In later years, after Gladys died, a lady called me and said nobody had a recording of her voice and I agreed to send her a copy of the interview for Vernon. I sent it by this lady and she gave it to Vernon. After he died, while they were cleaning out the closets at Graceland, somebody found the tape I had sent to Vernon. Somehow, RCA got it, but I wasn't consulted. My wife spent fifty dollars to buy that RCA album with a bit of my interview on it, but I still own the only original copy of that full interview.

Jimmy Angel
High-School Friend/Performer

During the '50s, Elvis and Pat Boone were the ones responsible for banging down the door for the black songwriters and helping get them onto mainstream radio. Anybody who picks up a guitar, from country to rock 'n' roll, should salute Elvis Presley and Pat Boone for their courage and foresight. Without them the black singers from Little Richard and Fats Domino to Jackie Wilson and many others would still be looking for a white radio station to push their music.

I first met Elvis at Humes High School. He was walking around with his guitar; all I did in high school was play ball and chase chicks. My mom and I lived in the Lauderdale Courts projects where Elvis lived when his family came to Memphis. Those project buildings were old with sawdust floors and that was where Elvis started. That boy started off like me and a few others: on a dirt floor, looking for food, trying to save money for food for his momma, daddy, and him—just like I was doing for Mom and me. From that poor start, he became "King of the World." Anytime I hear some of the guys goofing off on him or his music, I grab them and say, "Hey, cat, that was my friend; what do you do for a living that is so great?" It gets me very upset, and that is why I wrote "Let's Give the King a Rest" about the controversies and trials he had to overcome.

Elvis leaving New York and headed by train to Memphis after the *Ed Sullivan Show*.

"Man, he was something!"

Waylon Jennings

Al Wertheimer
Photographer

Talk about an interesting subject for a photographer. I had an assignment as a young professional in 1956 to observe and snap Elvis's RCA tour. It was only my first year in professional photography, so what did I know! The only thing I knew was that I had to make a living. But I became a messenger bringing seconds in time of Elvis's life to the world and recording his impact on others.

It was truly an education to observe Elvis Presley. I didn't like to talk to or direct my subjects. I was shy. Elvis didn't care to be talked to, he liked to direct, and he was shy too. We clicked. He permitted me closeness like no other I have ever photographed. I mean he allowed me to snap him only three feet away, as others would only allow six to eight feet. This guy never flinched. He didn't ham it up and he didn't pay attention to you. I would just go in there and get full image shots, changing the light and texture as I felt needed. That makes good photographs.

Elvis in Sheffield, Alabama, getting lunch during a train stop in the early to mid-'50s before becoming famous; no one recognized him.

The best experience was being there for his performances. He could make the girls cry. I don't know how he could make them cry. Elvis created such emotions with these girls that they'd keep hugging each other and crying until mascara ran down their faces. It was amazing. He was able to sing and reach out to the balcony and make the people in the balcony feel, "Oh, he is singing to me." Other singers can't do that. They sing to the first two rows and forget about the balcony. That is the genuine person of Elvis that you see.

***

A story about Elvis that sticks out takes place on a train headed from New York to Memphis. He gets up, and I get up and I don't know what he is doing. You can see he is thinking. Then he gets a cup of water, drinks it, throws the cup away, whirls around 180 degrees, and walks back in the direction from where he had come. I am just clicking one shot at a time. Not knowing what he is doing, I am saving my ammunition. He then goes halfway down the aisle, makes a sharp left turn, looks these two young ladies, ages

Elvis on a train from New York to Memphis.

fifteen and seventeen, in the face and he says, "You coming to my concert tonight?" They become befuddled: "Concert? Concert? Who are you?" Meantime, he has got this stuffed toy panda on his hip and he says, "Well, I'm Elvis Presley." And they say, "How do we know that?" Elvis says, "You see that photographer over there, standing on the seat? You think he would be taking my picture if I wasn't Elvis Presley?" That seemed to make a lot of sense to the girls and he went back to chatting them up and they wanted to be chatted up. So I went back to my seat in the front waiting for him to come up with another little scenario he could direct himself in.

Pat Boone
Singer/Actor

Elvis and I both knew we were a couple of "good ol' boys" from the south. We both had a sense that we had been blessed in unusual ways and talked some about what God's purpose might be in these blessings. I know from talking to his buddies, and from private conversations with Elvis himself, that he was on a spiritual quest. The only Grammy Awards he got while he was alive were for his gospel music, and he was seriously considering transforming his concerts into some kind of evangelical outreach—but I don't think his plans were fully developed before he died. I know it sounds bizarre, but Elvis proved he was perfectly willing to defy convention and do the unexpected. I've spent enjoyable hours trying to visualize an Elvis Presley altar call and what the results might have been. Apparently God had a different plan.

Elvis and cousin Billy Smith with unknown girl.

Jerry Schilling
Friend and Member of the Memphis Mafia

It was the Christmas of 1975. Elvis and I were upstairs in his room and Elvis wasn't feeling much like going down and doing his normal Christmas thing. He said, "I just don't feel like going downstairs this year." I said, "Then don't." There was a mix of friends and visitors downstairs. He didn't want to deal with the party so we just sat upstairs and talked for a while.

Later that evening he called his longtime Memphis jeweler Harry Levitch to come over because he wanted to get something for his grandma and for his dad, Vernon. He picked out something for his grandmother and then he decided on a ring for Vernon. I made out the check while Elvis talked with Harry privately.

After he left Elvis and I were alone again, and he sat down on the edge of the bed and picked up *Cheiro's Book of Numbers* and said, "I want to read you something, Jerry." He turned to a page he had marked and he told me, "You are a number six, Jerry. You know what that means?" I said, "No, E." So he read it to me

and asked me if that sounded like myself. I laughed and said that it was dead-on. "There's one more thing. It says a number six should always have an emerald close to his skin for well-being." He put the book down and reached in his pocket and pulled out a beautiful emerald ring and then he took my hand and slid the ring on. I asked him what number was he and he told me he was an eight and read what it said about an eight; it was a close description of him. When he finished, he smiled and said, "Merry Christmas, Six." "Merry Christmas, Eight," I answered.

Opposite: Elvis sailing to Hawaii for a much-needed vacation.

"Every time I saw Elvis tap into his creative abilities to take on some new kind of artistic challenge, I came away amazed again at the breadth of his talent."   Jerry Schilling

Elvis at the Audubon Drive house in Memphis, Tennessee, in 1956. Elvis recorded eight number-one songs while living there.

As Gordon Stoker of the Jordanaires listens, Ed Sullivan informs Elvis that he will only be filmed from the waist up for his televised performance on the *Ed Sullivan Show*.

Gordon Stoker
Manger and First Tenor, Jordanaires

I remember very well the night Elvis appeared on the *Ed Sullivan Show*. It was the number-one-rated show in America. Elvis was being paid the highest amount anyone had ever gotten for a TV spot. The show was being done live, and let me tell you, he was very much "uptight." We were as close behind him as possible on stage, and he was always stepping on our toes when he backed up. That is the main thing I remember about that evening: Elvis being very nervous. He could not remember the words on a couple songs, so he kind of depended on us to remember for him. If you note on "Love Me," he forgot the words going into the chorus and made up his words. He took liberties in the early years with songs and we as the Jordanaires helped cover up his forgetfulness. Elvis would even make faces at the camera. It was a lot of fun in those days. We have many great memories, that's for sure!

"Somehow I knew the entertainment world, and my life, would never be the same."

Jerry Chesnut

***Lonely Street*, by Ronnie McDowell, 1994**
Ronnie McDowell's first Elvis print features Elvis and James Dean coming together on Lonely Street. The title was inspired by the loneliness the two men experienced during their careers.

***Elvis and Friends,* by Ronnie McDowell, 2002**
In the original painting, Elvis was depicted in the studio with the
Jordanaires, guitarist Scotty Moore, drummer D.J. Fontana, and bassist
Bill Black as well as songwriter Jerry Leiber, seated at the piano, and
Judy Tyler, the lead actress with Elvis in the movie *Jailhouse Rock.*
McDowell replaced Jerry Leiber at the piano with Mike Curb, founder
of Curb Records and a great fan of Elvis, and presented the painting to
Curb as a Christmas present.

Ray Walker
Bass Singer, Jordanaires

The first time I saw Elvis, he walked into RCA Studios, came over to me and said, "I'm Elvis Presley." I responded, "I know who you are. I am Ray Walker," but he knew who I was. He was excited about meeting the bass singer the Jordanaires had picked up. When I looked at him, I saw that he had the best countenance about him when he talked to you. So when I looked at him he wasn't the famous Elvis Presley anymore. I saw the man inside.

Later in that session we were singing "A Fool Such As I." He was putting his fingers in my mouth and in my ear and pulling the back of my hair. I told him that with the heart he had he would go far in this business. He was a genuine person. Sometimes genuine people are misunderstood, but they don't go into hiding. He was distracted by his career, but he never went into hiding. He did so much for so many people and is still doing it. Genuine people are blessed. Elvis was blessed and his spirit still blesses us.

I will tell you one more thing. I was the morning disc jockey at WHLP, the Voice of Middle Tennessee, when his first record came out. I said then that his was the funniest name I had ever heard. People kept talking about him and asking was that his real name. Yes, it was Elvis Presley. I said, "Here he is, Elvis Presley. You may not like him but he is really going to be big!" There was already a big stir about him that came from the twenty- to fifty-year-old age group. But even children and the older folks all adored Elvis. There is the measure of a man; if the grandparents and the children love you, you're a winner. Children have no malice or contrived things in their hearts. They loved him. The old folks had lived long lives and didn't have to face the problems that he had, but they understood and they loved him for just being so real.

If he had been only in the church world, things might have been easier for Elvis. I was alone driving in my car through a storm when I heard on the radio that Elvis was dead at the age of forty-two. I've never felt him gone, not that day, not at the funeral, and not even today.

Opposite: Elvis recording "Hound Dog."

Elvis in Audubon Drive house in swim trunks as Gladys and his grandmother relax on the sofa.

"Mom was always my best girl."

Elvis Presley

Jerry Chesnut
Friend and Songwriter

I met Elvis through a mutual friend and so-called Memphis Mafia member Lamar Fikes. I knew I was being introduced to the King of Rock 'n' Roll and the entertainer of the century. This was the greatest thing that could happen to a songwriter like me, but I guess, to be perfectly honest, I have to say it was a somewhat disappointing experience. I'd had my songs recorded by Tom Jones, Brook Benton, George Jones, Johnny Cash, Loretta Lynn, Jerry Lee Lewis, and some of the greatest entertainers on earth, but this was different. This man was the Superman of the music world. I guess I expected some supernatural feeling, but the fact is, we shook hands and in a voice kind of like a little humble, shy, teenage boy, he asked, "How you doin'?" I don't remember how I answered.

In the next two or three years, I frequented Graceland, went to the movies and recording sessions, and took drives with him. It amazes me, to this day, looking back, how very simple and sincere true greatness can really be. He inspired me in my writing. Without thinking, I found myself trying to write great songs, not just hit songs.

Before the funeral, Vernon, Elvis's father, put a TCB (Taking Care of Business) necklace around my neck. Elvis had made it for me, the last one he commissioned before he died, and I stood and watched in disbelief as they opened his casket. He had released five of my songs and was learning another but suddenly he was gone. I remember him as nothing amazing, nothing supernatural, never trying to impress anyone, just a simple, wonderful, sweet American kid who never really had a chance to grow up. To me, this was and will always be Elvis.

A month before Elvis's death, he was seen at the Memphis, Tennessee, airport with Pat Boone.

"In the years since he's been gone, my life has been rich, eventful, and rewarding. And I don't ever forget that I've had a chance to live that kind of life because of the time I spent with Elvis." Jerry Schilling

George Klein
Friend and Disc Jockey

In 1968, just weeks before Christmas, Elvis sent a couple of the guys after me to go down to the local Cadillac dealership. It was late in the evening, after one of my radio shows, and we walked into the dealership. I thought Elvis was buying himself another car. Suddenly all the lights came on in the showroom and to my surprise, sitting in the middle of the floor was a brand-new yellow 1968 Cadillac convertible. I said, "Hey, Elvis, what's up?" and he said, "Come here. Stick out your right hand." I stuck out my right hand and he dropped the car keys in my hand and said, "Merry Christmas." I was overwhelmed! I turned to Elvis and said, "I should be able to make an Academy Award-winning speech since I am in radio, but I don't know what to say, man, 'cause nobody has ever given me a brand-new Cadillac." He just put his arm around me and said, "What is fame and fortune if you can't share it with your friends?"

Elvis with George Klein, his best man, at his wedding to Priscilla.

Elvis leaving Hudson Theatre, July 1, 1956.

Ronnie McDowell
Performer

To say that the connection between Elvis and me is coincidental would be an understatement. Our connection is almost mystical. You might even say it is a bit hair raising sometimes. Let me tell you about the Two Hairs.

In 1995, I was in Memphis to perform with the Memphis Symphony Orchestra for a celebration of what would have been Elvis's sixtieth birthday. I had just gotten out of the shower in preparation for the event. Steam filled the bathroom and the mirror was slightly fogged over. Before I wiped off the mirror something told me to gaze to the left-hand side of the sink. I stopped in mid-wipe and looked. I was mesmerized by what I saw. I got cold chills as my eyes looked upon two hairs lying side by side spelling out the prettiest E and P. I couldn't believe what I was seeing. It was as if Elvis was there and he had shaped the hairs into his initials.

I called Joe Meador, my manager, and Elvis's guitarist Scotty

Moore, who was also performing that night, and told them they had to come immediately to see something in my room. When they saw the letters on the side of the sink, the hairs on the back of their necks stood up. The picture that you see taken by Joe that night shows the hairs as exactly as they were found. Possibly a coincidence; read on.

After Elvis's birthday celebration that night, I returned to my room to sleep, but at 3 A.M., I was awakened by someone beating on my door. The hotel was on fire. I had time to grab my things

An untouched photo of the Two Hairs, taken by Joe Meador.

and from there I went to the Audubon House. At that time it was owned by a friend of mine, Mike Curb. The Audubon House was the first house that Elvis bought for himself and his family in Memphis before he bought Graceland for security reasons. During a stay there three years earlier, I had experienced something similarly mystifying in relation to Elvis.

When we returned to Nashville after the Two Hairs incident, a lady claiming to be a medium arrived at Joe's office and asked if Elvis had tried to contact me. Joe showed her the picture of the Two Hairs. She was very intrigued. She said that spirits performing physical manipulation was very rare but had great significance. Apparently, Elvis was working very hard to tell me something. She also said that Elvis was my guardian angel.

Through the years I have felt that to a certain extent she was correct. Projects concerning Elvis keep coming to me without my looking for them. Just hours after Elvis passed away, the late Lee Morgan and I co-wrote "The King Is Gone." I have lent my voice to several movies about Elvis Presley—*Elvis, Elvis and the Beauty Queen, Elvis and Me*—and was personally chosen by Priscilla Presley to do the music for ABC's 1990 television series

Ronnie McDowell and the Jordanaires performing "Love Me Tender" with Joe Meador on guitar at the gates of Graceland, televised live on CNN.

Elvis, about the early years of Elvis's career. I was also selected as the singing voice of Elvis for the 1997 Showtime TV special "Elvis Meets Nixon." It is as if Elvis is having a spiritual hand in it. For whatever reason, I'm deeply appreciative for the opportunity to be a part of keeping the memory of the King alive.

"He was an integrator; Elvis was a blessing. They wouldn't let black music through. He opened the door for black music."

Little Richard

The World's Greatest Rock and Roll Band: The Rising Sun Edition,
by Ronnie McDowell, 2007
This piece was originally painted in 1997 as a daytime scene featuring a
big Coca-Cola sign on the building. Sun Records owner Shelby Singleton
requested that I replace the Coca-Cola sign with a Sun label. "Now my
name will be forever connected with Sun, Elvis's first record label, and
with Elvis, and I'm real happy about that," says McDowell.

Judy Spencer Nelon
The Judy Nelon Group

Southern gospel music inspired the heart and music of Elvis from his early childhood. This love began at the First Assembly of God Church in Memphis, Tennessee, where with his beloved parents, Vernon and Gladys Presley, Elvis attended the home church of the famous Blackwood Brothers. During his boyhood, he often lacked enough money to buy tickets to the monthly all-night gospel sings, but he knew the groups he admired and had befriended would let him in the back door. It was here while watching the enthusiastic delivery of the southern gospel music style that he learned to shake his legs and curl his lips to the beat of the music. Jake Hess, the lead singer with the Statesmen Quartet who later founded the Imperials, was his favorite. The family requested Jake sing at his dear friend Elvis's Memphis funeral. The last record on Elvis's stereo the day he died was the new release from J.D. Sumner and the Stamps Quartet. The way gospel music touched Elvis was never more apparent than on the

documentary *He Touched Me: The Gospel Music of Elvis Presley,* when he asks J.D. and his quartet to sing "Sweet, Sweet Spirit" as he stands quietly listening with tears streaming down his face.

From the beginning, Elvis made sure he had gospel singers on his sessions. Gordon Stoker of the Jordanaires, Ben and Brock Speer, all of them were on his first RCA recordings in Nashville. He also included the gospel groups Imperials, J.D. Sumner and the Stamps Quartet, and a group he called Voice, with tenor Sherrill Nielson and Donnie Sumner, on his tours. After the shows Elvis would invite the singers to his suite where they would sing his favorite gospel songs for hours. "That was when Elvis's fun began," remembered Joe Moscheo of the Imperials.

***

Elvis, one of the most popular singers in the world, received fourteen Grammy nominations. Of those, he only won three Grammy Awards, all for gospel music: "How Great Thou Art" in 1967, "He Touched Me" in 1972, and his live Memphis recording of "How Great Thou Art" in 1974. In 1971, the National Academy of Recording Arts and Sciences recognized Elvis with a Lifetime Achievement Award, known then as the Bing Crosby Award in honor of its first recipient.

During his lifetime, Elvis sold millions of recordings, and since his death his sales have soared past the billion mark, according to RCA, his record label. In 2001, Elvis was inducted posthumously into the Gospel Music Association's Gospel Music Hall of Fame.

Priscilla Presley states in *Elvis by the Presleys,* "Gospel music was his deepest roots and, I believe, his deepest love."

"It's like he came along and whispered some dream in everybody's ear, and somehow we all dreamed it."

Bruce Springsteen

Elvis leaving concert at Russwood Park in Memphis.

Dak Alley
Singer/Songwriter, Actor, and Author

My Elvis story is probably like that of a lot of other Elvis fans.

I was on a family trip on my way back from California. We were on the outskirts of Las Vegas, Nevada, when I heard the news on the radio in my dad's camper: "Elvis Presley died today at the age of forty-two." Of course I was stunned, but I noticed that Dad was affected too. It was then I realized that Elvis really touched all ages. I said to Dad that we must have heard it wrong and that they must've meant that Elvis's dad, Vernon, had died, but then they started playing nothing but Elvis songs. By the time we got into Vegas, we knew there was no mistake. Elvis was really gone. I kept thinking that this couldn't be true. Elvis was bigger than life! I knew they hadn't made a mistake, so I wanted to believe that maybe he faked his death.

Yeah, like a lot of fans, I was ready to believe that he faked his death rather than deal with the reality that he was gone. Then, what seemed like only a few days later, I heard a song on the radio called the "King Is Gone." Then I knew it, Elvis had to have faked his death. No one could sound that close to Elvis and not be him.

Well, I was wrong. Ronnie McDowell, whom we would later know as a great country music artist with a lot of great songs in his own career, was singing this tune. Yes, he did sound a lot like Elvis. Little did I know that much later the idea that Elvis had faked his death would stick in my head and with the help of Elvis's cousin Edie Hand and my wife, LA Marie, I would come to write a book based on that very subject thirty years later. That same great singer who'd had me convinced that Elvis was still alive would also record one of my songs about Elvis, Martin Luther King, and B.B. King called "The Kings of Memphis." It's funny how life comes at you sometimes.

That's one of my Elvis memories. Although I did like hangin' out with him in Vegas! Oh, that's right, that part didn't happen—or did it?

"When Elvis came to the Grand Ole Opry for a visit, word trickled through the halls that he was in the building. He was dressed in a tuxedo. He was extremely handsome and very polite. He said hello to everyone, came over to me and my family, and introduced himself. He returned later to talk with me and dance and gave me a kiss on the cheek as he left. He was so nice to everyone. It was certainly an incredible experience."

Carol Lee Cooper

Opposite: Elvis at Penn Station in New York.

Terry Blackwood
Singer, Imperials

I remember a story about Elvis and my family from even before I met him or sang with him. Elvis was a big Blackwood Brothers and Statesmen Quartet fan, and he sure did love the once-a-month gospel singings at Ellis Auditorium in Memphis. He came quite often and met all the Blackwoods, including my daddy.

Elvis had already begun to establish himself as a star with several hits in 1956. That year my daddy, Doyle, decided to run for the state legislature and received the nomination for that office in Memphis. He was told there would be a big parade down Main Street in Memphis on a certain a date. He needed a convertible for the parade. We didn't own one so Daddy called Elvis and asked him if he would let him use one of his convertibles for the big parade. Elvis said sure, and he was most gracious to Daddy. Finally, the big parade down Main Street in Memphis, Tennessee, arrived for our family. My parents, with

Opposite: Elvis besieged by fans at the back door of Studio 50 in New York.

my sister and I in the back seat, rode down Main Street in the only pink Cadillac convertible. It is a great memory of the way I began to know of Elvis Presley's generosity.

"I love Elvis Presley's music because he was my generation. But then again, Elvis is everyone's generation."

Margaret Thatcher

Elvis relaxing behind Audubon Drive house drinking a Pepsi, his favorite soda.

John Hughey
Steel Guitar Player

I met Elvis Presley in 1956 in Memphis, Tennessee, when I was playing with Slim Rhodes and his band. I was the steel guitar player. We played all over the Mid-South. We had a good gig at the Memphis Mid-South Fair at about the time that Elvis was really getting noticed with lots of air play of his songs "Blue Moon of Kentucky" and "That's All Right (Mama)." Well, as luck would have it, he came strolling through the fairgrounds and stopped to hear our band. Naturally, Slim recognized him and called him up from the audience to sing a couple of songs with our band. I remember he was dressed so casually, with faded blue jeans and a white T-shirt with the sleeves torn out. He was something!

Later I went to work with Conway Twitty, and while we were touring in Maryland my wife called me and asked, "Would you like to do an album with Elvis?" I said, "Lord yeah." I think it was about 1970 when she booked me. We recorded two albums with Elvis, "From Elvis in Memphis" and "Elvis Back in Memphis" at

American Studios. He was just a nice guy and would walk around putting his arm around folks and telling them what a good job they were doing.

Another experience with Elvis was after he had really gotten big and started working in Las Vegas. I was actually playing in Vegas with Conway Twitty about twice a month and Elvis would invite us all to come see his show. He always invited us back to his dressing room to visit after his show. Elvis was just as straight as an arrow and a wonderful human being that I was fortunate to get to know.

Howard Hite
Tupelo Hardware Company

Tupelo Hardware in Tupelo, Mississippi, was founded in 1926 by George H. Booth and is still owned and managed by generations of the Booth family. We are an old hardware store and we are famous for a lot of things, and one of them is selling Elvis his first guitar.

Actually, it was his mother who bought that first guitar here in Tupelo. Elvis came into our store in 1945 with his mother, Gladys, to buy Elvis a bicycle. When they entered the store, they came through the same front door that we have here right now, and they walked on the same floor that is here, and they went to the counter that is now known as our Elvis counter. Elvis stopped there because he had seen a .22 rifle that was hanging on the wall right behind that counter, and Elvis decided that he wanted the rifle instead of the bicycle that they had come to buy. But his mother said, "No, you're not going to have the rifle," so little ten-year-old Elvis got upset because his mama wouldn't buy him the rifle.

Tupelo Hardware Company, Inc. ESTABLISHED IN 1920

•••••••••••••• Hardware Distributors •••

WILLIAM T. BOOTH
VICE PRESIDENT-SECRETARY

FRONT & MAIN STREET
BOX 1040 — PHONE 601 842-4637
Tupelo, Mississippi 38801
OCTOBER 2, 1979

GOOD MORNING--------
MY NAME IS FORREST L. BOBO. MY HOME ADDRESS IS
607 SOUTH CHURCH STREET, TUPELO, MISSISSIPPI. I
AM 78 YEARS YOUNG TODAY, BUT I CAN WELL REMEMBER
THE AFTERNOON WHEN ELVIS PRESLEY AND HIS MOTHER CAME
INTO THE TUPELO HARDWARE, WHERE I WORKED FOR TWENTY
YEARS. HE WANTED TO BUY A 22 CAL. RIFLE AND HIS
MOTHER WANTED HIM TO BUY A GUITAR. I SHOWED HIM THE
RIFLE FIRST AND THEN I GOT THE QUITAR FOR HIM TO
LOOK AT. I PUT A WOOD BOX BEHIND THE SHOWCASE AND
LET HIM PLAY WITH THE GUITAR FOR SOMETIME. THEN HE
SAID HE DID NOT HAVE THAT MUCH MONEY, WHICH WAS ONLY
$7.75 PLUS A 2% SALES TAX. HIS MOTHER TOLD HIM THAT
IF HE WOULD BUY THE GUITAR INSTEAD OF THE RIFLE,
SHE WOULD PAY THE DIFFERENCE FOR HIM. THE PAPERS
HAVE SAID THAT THE GUITAR COST $12.50 BUT AT THAT
TIME, YOU COULD HAVE BOUGHT A REAL NICE ONE FOR THAT
AMOUNT. THE SMALL AMOUNT OF MONEY THAT HE HAD TO
SPEND HAD BEEN EARNED FROM RUNNING ERRANDS AND DOING
SMALL JOBS FOR PEOPLE.

I AM PROUD TO HAVE A LITTLE PART IN ELVIS' LIFE. I
HAD SUPPER WITH ELVIS THE NIGHT HE LEFT FOR HIS FIRST
AUDITION. WE ALL WISHED HIM A GREAT SUCCESS, AND HE
SURE MADE A GREAT LIFE FOR HIMSELF AND THE REST OF
THE WORLD.

THANK YOU FOR YOUR TIME.

Forrest L. Bobo

FORREST L. BOBO

There was a longtime employee who was standing behind the counter and working with Elvis and his mother, and his name was Forrest Bobo. Mr. Bobo was trying to think of something to calm Elvis down, and there just happened to be a guitar in that counter, on the top shelf. So Mr. Bobo opened the door, he reached in and pulled the guitar out, and he told Elvis, "Here, try this guitar." So Elvis took the guitar and he strummed it and played with it a little bit, and his mother said, "Elvis, I'll buy you the guitar if you'll take the guitar." So Elvis played the guitar for a few more minutes, and he turned back to his mother and he said, "Yes, ma'am, I'll take the guitar." And of course, the rest is absolute history.

I think that we feel that Tupelo Hardware Company played a part in the musical history of Elvis Presley and rock 'n' roll. I like to think of Elvis's birthplace as being the cradle of rock 'n' roll, and I like to think of Tupelo Hardware as quick starting rock 'n' roll at a young age, because as we all know, Elvis Presley grew up to be the King of Rock 'n' Roll.

We still sell guitars, about 450 guitars a year. I have had a lot of celebrities come through the store—well, we have twenty-five to

thirty thousand people come through the store. I've had Ronnie McDowell, who is a very famous singer that's been in our store, I've had Joe Perry with Aerosmith that's been in the store, and all these people come here because of Elvis. Pam Tillis, who is a country singer—I don't know if she lives in Nashville or not, but she's very famous—Mel Tillis's daughter. We had the Crown Prince of Monaco, Prince Albert, who is Grace Kelly and Prince Rainier's son, and he is a huge Elvis fan. He and his entourage came in here unannounced. I told them the same story that I just told you. We just like what we did, and we think with Gladys buying Elvis his first guitar here, it truly put us on the map, and it probably helped Elvis's career get kick-started.

Opposite: **Reflection of a King***, by* **Ronnie McDowell, 2008**
A ten-year-old Elvis glimpses his future as he looks in the mirror at the house where he was born in Tupelo, Mississippi.

Gladys bought Elvis his first guitar from Tupelo Hardware.

Edie Hand
Family Member

It was always hot at our Hood/Hacker home for the Fourth of July celebrations. Grandma Alice had cat head biscuits in the oven and fried catfish with hush puppies in her big iron skillets. I can still smell her kitchen today! Grandpa Hacker had big pots of stew brewing outside with his kinfolks bringing the side dishes and lots of desserts.

Even with all this, nothing was as exciting as making music on the front porch with my mother Sue's brothers' families and their friends. I tell you, I come from a tribe of folks. There were twelve children in Walter and Alice Hood Hacker's family and they were all talented. If you couldn't sing or play an instrument, Grandma would bring out the spoons. You see, our family had a great heritage in music, our claim to fame was our cousin Elvis Presley. Grandma Alice was daughter to Harrison Hood, who was Minnie Mae Hood Presley's brother. Now that is a mouthful.

At one special reunion, Uncle Vernon brought Grandma

Alice Hood Hacker, Elvis's aunt, held Fourth of July family reunions in Russellville, Alabama, with occasional visits from Elvis, his father Vernon, and his grandmother Minnie Mae Hood Presley. Here the family makes music on the front porch of Hacker's home.

Minnie to visit because our Great-Granddad Harrison Hood was very ill with diabetes. I can still see him sitting on the front porch surveying the drive in his wheelchair. He would clap his hands with joy to see that long black car with the Presleys drive up to join the family reunion. Elvis would come later that night to visit Grandpa Hood. What a hoedown we had, with all-day singing, food on the blankets, and I'm sure whiskey in the bushes with a little bit of devilment around. A true setting for generations of varied talents to spring from at an Alabama family reunion that was fit for the King of Memphis.

Twilight Magic, by Ronnie McDowell, 2000. Originally titled *The Sumner County Drive-In,* 1994-1998

In 1956, the Elvis movie *Love Me Tender* saved the owners of the Sumner County Drive-In, Mr. and Mrs. Smith, from going bankrupt. Everyone loved a Saturday night movie with Elvis.

Acknowledgments

A very special thank-you to the people who helped create this book:

Al Wertheimer
Louise Smith
Mike Curb
Dick Clark
Shelby Singleton
Charlie Watts
George Klein
Gordon Stoker
Howard Hite
Pat Boone
Foster Carter
Bill Flannery
Sharon Anderton
Keith Dunn

Sally Meador
Mark Aldridge
the team at Pelican Publishing Company

MEET THE AUTHORS
Ronnie McDowell, Edie Hand, and Joe Meador

Ronnie McDowell has amassed an amazing string of hit songs over the years, but it is his riveting stage presence and genuine warmth that fill the seats again and again. Like all great entertainers, he has a personality that remains luminous long after the lights go dim. These qualities have inspired a nationwide network of fan clubs with a total of more than three thousand members, each one a devoted promoter of everything Ronnie does.

Following the death of Elvis Presley in 1977, Ronnie came out of nowhere to dazzle the world with his heartfelt and self-penned tribute song, "The King Is Gone," on the independent Scorpion label. The record found airplay on country and pop stations across the country and around the world and has sold

more than five million copies. The song's impact was so great that it landed McDowell guest appearances on numerous radio and television programs, including WSM's *Grand Ole Opry* and Dick Clark's *American Bandstand.*

Two of Ronnie's more recent projects on Curb Records include an album of beach music with Rock and Roll Hall of Famer Bill Pinkney's Original Drifters entitled, cleverly enough, "Ronnie McDowell with Bill Pinkney's Original Drifters." The second project is a country album titled "Ronnie McDowell Country," a collection of six original McDowell-penned songs and a few country standards by such legendary writers as Buck Owens, Harlan Howard, and Dallas Frazier. Both projects were produced by McDowell.

He is constantly in demand as a performer, and he tours relentlessly with his band, the Rhythm Kings. Additionally, he often tours with Elvis Presley original sidemen Scotty Moore and D. J. Fontana, along with Millie Kirkham and the Jordanaires, as a tribute to Elvis Presley's music.

Ronnie sang thirty-six songs on the soundtrack for *Elvis,* the Dick Clark-produced television movie that featured Kurt Russell as the legendary performer. He also was the singing voice for the television movie *Elvis and the Beauty Queen,* the movie *Elvis and Me,* the ABC television series about the early years of Elvis's career titled simply *Elvis,* as well as the 1997 Showtime special "Elvis Meets Nixon." While Elvis Presley has played a big part in McDowell's music career over the years, Ronnie continues to entertain audiences with his own blend of romantic intimacy and honky-tonk excitement.

Edie Hand is one of those remarkable people who brightens up a room as she walks in. Her philosophy for living life with gusto can be seen in everything she does, from her work as an acclaimed celebrity chef to author-philanthropist, speaker, and businesswoman. Strongly influenced by her modest childhood growing up in the rural south as a member of the extended Presley family, Edie embraces the simple joys of family and helping others in times of need.

Edie has starred in national commercials and daytime television soap operas. She was CEO of her own advertising agency for over twenty years and was recognized in the '80s as a young and rising advertising executive. An alumni of the University of North Alabama, Edie is involved in professional and humanitarian organizations. She lives with her husband, Mark Aldridge, near Birmingham, Alabama. Her only son, Line Hand, lives in Los Angeles, California.

Joe Meador began his professional music career in his native Kentucky. In his three decades in the music industry, he has toured all across America with such artists as Ricky Nelson and Frankie Valli and the Four Seasons. He has managed Ronnie McDowell, Hank Williams III, Submethod, co-managed Six Shooter, and currently manages Wayd Battle, Kyhil, and Zack Tyson. Joe has written songs for George Strait,

Ronnie McDowell, and Jerry Lee Lewis, just to mention a few. He has produced CDs and worked on movie soundtracks and award-winning documentaries. Since 1994, he has been president and CEO of Grand Entertainment Group in Nashville, which consists of a top management company and six publishing companies. Because of his vast experience in the music and business side of the industry, Joe is well respected in the music community, and his reputation is one of honesty and integrity. Joe has a strong commitment to innovation, and his creativity for scouting talent in the music world has lent itself to cutting-edge development projects.